Seeking Balance In
an Unbalanced Time

Steven Greenebaum

For information, contact
MSI Press
1760-F Airline Highway, #203
Hollister, CA 95023

Cover designed by Carl Leaver
Cover Photograph by ShutterStock
Author Photo on Back Cover by Kevin Clark/The Herald

Copyeditor: Van Wolverton

Library of Congress Number: 2020941032

ISBN: 978-1-950328-36-9

Contents

Steven Greenebaum

A Family In Crisis

Pandemic. For most of us, and I certainly include myself, the notion of a worldwide pandemic has been ripped out of the realm of the theoretical and dumped with a thud in our laps. What do we do? How do we cope? How on Earth do we cope? How do we even try to lead some version of normal lives when life is no longer normal? How can we find and keep some kind of balance as we walk this pandemic tightrope? These are tough, important questions—and we want answers. Living a life of uncertainty 24/7 can break our heart and our spirit. Everything seems out of balance, especially our lives. So, what do we do?

The honest truth is, of course, there's no one answer that solves this. There are so many different things for us to deal with as we try to keep our balance. What I'd like to do is offer what may be only a partial answer, but one I think we can hold onto. Speaking as a retired Interfaith minister, what I'll ask us grapple with in the pages that follow is how we might deal with what can seem like an overwhelming challenge to our spiritual and emotional health. No, we can't rid ourselves of the stress. But I do believe that by working to steady our equilibrium we can keep ourselves from being overwhelmed. Ok, fine! Just how do we find this emotional and spiritual balance? How do we deal with the uncertainties we face – the separations that confront us and the very real dangers that stare back at us in the night?

For me, I've always found that tough problems are made at least a smidge easier by breaking them down into somewhat smaller pieces. I'd ask us to look at four of these pieces. The first is this chapter—the whole picture, if you will—looking at the pandemic, not as a personal crisis, nor a national crisis, but a family crisis, a crisis the whole of our human family faces.

Our family? Really? Yes! We live in a hugely divisive time. You may have noticed. We divide by race, by religion, by ethnicity, by gender, and, with very firm lines on our maps, by nation. This COVID-19 pandemic recognizes none of these divisions; and for us right now, it's particularly important to remember it respects no borders. A virus that started in China has made its way all over the world. And it may well again. What happens not only in the United States but in Africa, Europe, Russia, Asia, South America, indeed what happens *everywhere* should concern us not only because we are one with our human family, but because this virus ignores all borders. It may well leave and then come back.

Seeking Balance In an Unbalanced Time

Okay, so the crisis is huge and involves all of humanity. Now what? Let's leave politics for others to deal with. Surely there's plenty of time and space for "the blame game" elsewhere. What I'd like to look at is, recognizing that this is indeed a crisis affecting the entirety of our human family, what do we do? What can you do? What can I do? What can the communities we live in do?

I believe it is crucial for us to understand that a time of crisis does not define who we are. The pandemic does *not* define us. The truth of it is, it is in a time of crisis that our facades slip and we truly reveal ourselves. A time like this strips away our illusions. What we proclaim becomes meaningless. How we act is who we are. So, while we shelter in place or find ourselves outside of our home (at least from time to time), and then as we try to cope as the world slowly opens again, what we do or do not do will define not only who we are but also who we will be. A time of crisis strips away who we hope to be and leaves us alone with who we are. So, the question becomes, what action will we take? What will we do?

That's a hard one! The truth of it is, depending on how we say it, "What can I do?" can either be a cry of despair or a cry of empowerment. Truly. "What can *I* do?" is a cry of despair. The problem is so huge, we feel powerless. But "What can I *do*?" is a cry of empowerment. "I cannot do everything, but I can do something." is a wonderful statement of empowerment from Rev. Edward Everett Hale (full quote in the Appendix).

I believe one of the most important things we can do to keep our sanity and our spiritual balance is not allow ourselves to get lost in the crisis. And one of the best ways not to get lost is to embrace Rev. Hale's approach to put aside regret about what we can't do and embrace what we can. It has always helped me to think of what I can do in terms of cards that I am playing in a game. Whether it's bridge, or poker, or some other card game, what truly matters are the cards we hold. Wishing we had a better hand is pointless. The cards we have are the only cards we can play. So, the question in this pandemic, as in all of life, is "What are my cards?"

Now in my seventies, I've learned to enlarge the card analogy. There were things I could do when I was thirty that became a lot harder in my fifties, and are in truth no longer possible in my seventies. I think of me in my thirties as holding one set of cards. The cards I held in my fifties were different. The cards that I hold now are very different. As we play our hands in this game of life, whatever the stage of our lives, what matters is our answer to the question: "What cards do I hold now?" It's very human to mourn cards that we could once play but no longer hold, or cards we wish we had but don't. I've done it. More than once I've mourned the cards I don't have, but never have I found it to be helpful. Isn't asking, "What cards can I play?" more positive and spiritually rewarding than, "What cards have I lost?"

It's up to each one of us to determine how to play the hand we've been dealt. So, I wouldn't dream of trying to tell you how you should play your hand. But whatever our hand, we are so much freer to play the cards we have when we aren't distracted by frustration over the cards we don't (though this in no way means we shouldn't work to improve the hands our children will have!). And if someone we know has "better" cards, let him or her play them. We'll play the cards we've got. And if we keep our balance, we can play them to the very best of our ability.

Balance. Why do I keep harping on balance? It's because in this "either/or" world we much too often inhabit, we can frequently find ourselves pulled toward one extreme or another. Either this, or that. Nothing in between. We seek balance because if we are blown off balance we can find ourselves stuck at one extreme or the other. And being stuck, by definition, means we become immobile.

One destructive set of polar opposites that has been particularly in evidence during the pandemic are fear and denial. Some of us have surrendered to fear. Yes, COVID-19 can indeed be deadly. The death-toll can be staggering. But we are not all going to die. And yes, many of us have lost our jobs. But hopefully our government will act, and those who have lost their jobs will receive the support they need to keep it together until this is over. And the truth of it is that all pandemics, no matter how deadly and destructive, end. They do end! Our economies will come back, they always have. So, if we would keep our balance and keep from being overwhelmed, we want to identify paralyzing fear as an obstacle to our well-being, be willing to grapple with it, and strive to leave it in the dust.

The polar opposite of fear is denial. The truth of it is there are folks among us, even now, who dwell in the house of denial. After all, at one point the president said this was just the flu and would vanish. Poof: gone! Several prominent radio commentators have gone farther, one even calling it the common cold. Given how many around the world and in the United States have been infected and how many have died and continue to die, it's hard to imagine how someone could still cling to the belief that COVID-19 is just a simple flu, let alone the common cold; but that's the power of denial. And when people have embraced denial it can be all but impossible to coax them away from it. Facts become meaningless.

Fear and denial can both immobilize us. Yet, both tug at us. So, we'll want to keep our balance between the two.

Okay. So, what else needs to be balanced in order for us to do what we can, given the cards we hold? For one thing, we need a balance of attention between us and the world outside. That's what we'll begin discussing in Chapter Two. We all know folks who think of themselves and only themselves. That's just plain unhealthy, not to mention narcissistic and hurtful. This is how families are ripped apart and destroyed. But we also know folks who think only of others, putting everyone else first and themselves last. This is also unhealthy, as never taking care of ourselves puts us at risk. The truth is, in order to be healthy enough to help others, we must also take care of ourselves. Again, we'll explore this more deeply in Chapter Two with some thoughts on a nurturing healthy regard for ourselves.

In Chapter Three we'll explore the needs of our human family, and what we might do for our brothers and sisters. I deeply believe in humanity as a family. Indeed, I wrote a book about it (*One Family: Indivisible*), sharing why I believe so strongly that we are all brothers and sisters and how I came to that belief. So again, if we always put ourselves or even our personal family first, to the exclusion of our brothers and sisters around the world, we have lost our balance.

There's one final aspect to our balancing act that I'd like us to examine. This is balance between today and tomorrow. In the midst of the pandemic it's hard, very hard to think of anything past how we survive today—how do we pay the rent or mortgage, how do we keep food on the table, how do we stay healthy? These are huge and important questions! But if we can somehow maintain a bit of balance, we might just make for a better future. I believe that one of the reasons we are so deeply in this mess today is the fact that in the past, too many in positions of power were only thinking and spending for their today, not giving enough thought to the tomorrow that we are now living. No matter what happens with the pandemic, and no matter when it ends, it will end. And from that ending will come a "new normal." In Chapter Four, we'll take a brief look at how we might begin to envision and work for a positive "new normal."

Doing for Ourselves

I don't know if we're born with it or pick it up as children, but I strongly believe that how we see others as opposed to ourselves develops early. Some of us are oriented to think of others first and ourselves second if at all. Then again, some of us are oriented to think of ourselves first and others second if at all. There's a spectrum here, a big one, and I'm not going to offer an opinion as to which point on that spectrum is "best" or where we "should" seek to be. The truth of it is in times of great stress, we can all find ourselves pushed toward one extreme or the other. Some of us may think only of others. Others may think only of ourselves. As we've seen, both extremes lack balance. So, for the next two chapters we'll explore some healthy ways to achieve a balance: making the effort to have what we do for ourselves not be in conflict with what we do for others. Doing both for ourselves and others is what helps to make us whole. They are in no way mutually exclusive.

Some will tell us that doing for ourselves is selfish. I would agree that if I only take care of myself, if I only consider myself in how I act, I am indeed being selfish. Yet, it is also true that if I continually ignore my own needs and refuse to look out for myself in my day-to-day activities, I put both my spiritual and physical health in danger. I cleave to a quote from Rabbi Hillel, "If I am not for myself, who will be for me? Yet, if I am only for myself, what am I? And if not now, when?" What Hillel calls for is balance—while reminding us that there's no time like the present.

So, what might we do for ourselves in this time of working under huge stress, if indeed we have work, as well as sheltering in place and social distancing? I don't pretend to have "the answer," but I would like to share some practices I have found helpful in keeping myself whole. Perhaps they'll be useful. And if some or all of these practices are not useful, perhaps they'll prompt the reader to come up with practices that will work for them, and indeed help them maintain both balance and spiritual health.

First up: every morning, when I open my window shades, I look outside, rain or shine, and say, "Hello, world!" There *is* a world out there. No matter what else is happening, there is a whole huge world out there, and greeting it helps me. When I say, "Hello, world," I say it out loud. We will all have differing views from our bedroom window. I'm lucky enough to have a pear tree I planted growing right outside my window. Frequently, there's a bird flying by or a squirrel running along the fence. Saying "hello" to the trees, to the birds, to the squirrels, and to the world helps to reconnect me. It's an important part of consciously centering myself before the day takes off.

Another part of centering myself is my morning coffee ritual. I'll leave it to psychologists to explain why it's true, but I will share that I find rituals wonderfully comforting. Rituals can help to center us, adding order and warmth to the disordered and frequently cold world of stress—whether that stress comes from sheltering in place, actions or inactions by politicians, or the even more stressful wondering if we will have a job or money for food. Rituals are not an answer. Rituals will not rid us of the pandemic. What they can do is provide a measure of comfort in uncomfortable times. I believe that's an important reason why every one of our spiritual traditions include a raft of rituals.

My coffee ritual does that for me. I have collected a lot of mugs over the years, but every morning, there is one and only one mug that I use for my coffee—and I use it only for coffee. If later on in the day I have some tea, I'll use a different mug. Keeping one mug just for coffee helps me get my day started in a positive direction. Yeah, go figure. But it works!

A quick aside. My morning ritual coffee mug is a "Notorious RBG" mug with a picture of Justice Ginsberg on it. Ruth and I have had some great talks over coffee though I should admit that I talk and she listens. Beyond the fun, what's important here is that there is no one "right" mug. Frankly, you may not feel like talking with Justice Ginsberg in the morning. Where rituals can become toxic is if I take what works for me and insist not only that my ritual is "right" and will work for you but also that any differing ritual you might try is "wrong." So, I'm not suggesting you copy what I do. What I am strongly suggesting is that each of us find a morning ritual that works for us, helps to comfort and center us, and allows us to greet the new day with a smile, not fear.

And if you happen to have a Facebook page, you might also consider this. Every morning (time of day depending on when I get up!), I post a "Good morning, world!" It's a positive, and for me, wonder-filled post, a picture centered on nature and the beauty the world we live in can indeed hold for us—if we will pause long enough to take the time and look. There's nothing negative and nothing lengthy in these posts. Having said hello to the natural world when I opened my blinds, what I seek out and post here is a friendly "hello" to humankind and particularly my Facebook friends. In order to pull this off every morning, I'm always on the lookout for positive, wonderfully attractive posts about this planet we live on, and then save them to use as they call to me in the morning. It helps both to center me and start my day in a good frame of mind.

But how to deal with the stress-filled, often crazy day that we encounter? Specifically, for me, how do I come to the end of the day, no matter how difficult that day, without throwing something, or screaming, or climbing into bed at night with my mind aflame with anger or hurt or both? Every evening I post an "Evening smile" before signing off of Facebook. Sometimes it's wordplay (ok, truth is I'm an incorrigible punster), sometimes it's a funny "gif". The idea is never, ever to end the day without a smile. And again, this forces me to go searching for a post somewhere that evokes a smile and when I find it, save it to be used as it calls to me for an "evening smile" depending on my mood. The hunt for the evening smile itself is wonderfully therapeutic.

Making it a spiritual practice to start every day with the wonder of planet Earth (and for at least that moment shutting out the sadness and hardships), including in that spiritual practice a morning ritual that comforts and centers, and then ending every day with a smile (no matter how frustrated or angry events of the day may have made me) really helps me to keep my spiritual balance. I refuse to ignore what is happening in the world, which is why, while I am careful not to end my day with a scream, I sometimes let out a rather strong yelp somewhere mid-day. But starting with a wonder and a comforting ritual and ending with a smile, these help to keep my spiritual house in order. I strongly recommend it.

Staying balanced during the day can be somewhat more difficult (which is why I am sometimes prone to curse a bit mid-day). And frankly, some days are a lot harder than others. Still, there is one thing I consciously do during the day. I want to listen to enough of the news to be informed. I deeply believe that the old saying is wrong. Ignorance isn't bliss. Igno-

rance is deadly. On the other hand, I make it a point
to turn off the news once I know what is happening
and find other things to fill what is at the moment
my socially distanced, shelter-in-place day. Reading
is good. Watching old favorite movies is good. But
for me, more enjoyable than that is reaching for the
telephone. I recommend it. More about this in the
next chapter, but I believe it is truly important that
socially distanced *not* become translated into socially
isolated. I remember from my youth (you know, some
sixty years ago!) a slogan from Ma Bell (if you don't
know who she was, have some fun and web-search
her!): "Reach out and touch someone."

A healthy spiritual practice, however, needs to be
more than starting the day with wonder, not watching
toooo TOOO much news, and ending with a smile. So,
let me share a few more spiritual practices. Some may
work for you. Some may not. The point is not that I
believe you should adopt what I do (though if it works
for you, welcome to it), but rather I do believe that
each of us needs to embrace with intention a spiritual practice to both nurture and heal our stressed out
selves. So, what else helps?

After I've posted "Good morning, world!" and
checked up on what my friends are up to, I like to deal
with three specific questions to start the day rolling.

1) What can I do for me – today?

2) What can I do for my family and friends – today?

3) What can I do for my human family – today?

Seeking Balance In an Unbalanced Time

I have long accepted that from time to time the answer to one or more of these questions may be "Nothing." But if I answered "Nothing" to a question yesterday, I try to make darn sure to address it today. And the honest truth of it is, it's not so much answering the questions as it is asking them that helps to keep us centered.

There's one other thing, so obvious that I almost forgot about it: exercise! If you can get outside, go for it! Enjoy nature. Hike. Walk. Ride your bicycle. And for those of us who must shelter-in-place, in these socially distanced days it's indoor exercise. I feel fortunate in that I bought what I call my "bike to nowhere" (an indoor bicycle) years ago. I'll turn on the TV (and if there's nothing worth watching, put on a DVD) and peddle from four to nine "miles" on my bike (depending on that day's energy level) at least four times a week. It has replaced my four times a week half hour mall-walk with a friend that is currently out of the question. But if a bike to nowhere is unavailable, there are other forms of exercise, and some TV shows involve exercise. Again, it's not how we exercise, it's that we make the time and effort to be sure our bodies get some kind of a workout at least every other day. Exercise itself may or may not seem like fun, but once we've exercised our bodies really appreciate it. And so does our ability to balance.

One last thought on doing for ourselves. We all make mistakes. From time to time (or in times of stress even more often), we can feel alone—alone and unimportant. Stress does that. As mentioned above,

I deeply believe that we are one family—the human family. That makes us all brothers and sisters. I'm a great fan of Gilbert and Sullivan, but I have to disagree with a quote from their operetta: "The Gondoliers". "When everybody's somebody, then no one's anybody." No thank you (and in fairness, Gilbert and Sullivan loved satire). My quote would be, "When everybody's somebody, then we're finally making some progress!"

Each of us is somebody and an important part of our human family. But I'll confess, Max Ehrmann said it much better (full quote in the Appendix):

"You are a child of the universe, no less than the trees and the stars; you have a right to be here."

Whoever and wherever you are, you matter. I know this for a fact because every human being on this planet matters. Not only you and I, but all the rest of our human family has a right to be here as well. How can we help? Let's move on to the next chapter, "Doing for Others".

3

Doing for Others

Remembering the words of Hillel, "If I am not for myself, who will be for me? Yet if I am only for myself, what am I?" In this time of crisis, if we would not be only for ourselves, a question we want to ask is what is open to us to help our brothers and sisters? This will be a slightly shorter chapter; not because doing for others is any less important than doing for ourselves, but because to a large extent, what we do for others depends on our own spiritual health (doing for ourselves) and the cards we have. So now we want to look at how might we constructively examine the cards we have and ask what are some positive avenues for playing them?

I suppose I could launch into a pointed and passionate statement on the topic of what it says about a person when they are billionaires and remain a billionaire with a world in crisis and so many in need. But the truth of it is I'm not a billionaire and you prob-

ably aren't either, and for me one of the great paralyzing forces within our culture is our fixation on what
someone else is doing, or not doing – in this case, billionaires. One of the most important spiritual experi-
ences I had as a youth was a time when I was faced,
along with a lot of other youths in my school, with
an oppressive teacher. I kept wondering "Why doesn't
someone DO something?" And for the first time it
echoed back at me, "You're someone, why don't you
do something?" Ever since, I've never been able to ask
"Why doesn't someone do something?" without asking myself what I'm going to do. So, let's forget the
billionaires for now. What are **we** going to do?

I have some wonderful friends. One friend is
spending a lot of time in her car taking food from
food banks and delivering it to people who can't come
to a food bank. I have another friend who helps staff
a food bank, handing out packages of food to people
who have been in line, sometimes for hours, hoping
for some help feeding their families. I have another
friend who has training as a counselor and is now on-
line offering free virtual help to people who need it. I
have another friend who cannot sew, but seeing the
need for all of us to have some kind of mask when
we go out, and seeing that there were a lot of people
in her area willing to sew masks but having no idea
how to distribute them, decided that where she could
help was in organizing. She got friends who could put
a website together, made calls to others who knew
where the masks were needed, and created an inter-
net hub where people who sewed masks could con-

tact people who could deliver masks, and people who could deliver masks could find out where they were needed.

What each of these friends did was examine what cards they held and how they might use them. I love and salute these dedicated friends. However, the truth of it is, I don't hold the same cards they do. I'm seventy-two, with a heart condition (I've had triple bypass surgery) and have just come off my third (successful!) battle with cancer. I don't have a lot of energy right now. On top of that, I have arthritis in both my hands that severely limits what I can do. As an example, my driving is limited, and while I used to help out at the food bank, that's off the table as well. But what I truly want to stress is that what is important is not what I can't do, but what I can. I love my friends. I admire my friends, and all my brothers and sisters in my home city, as well as my state, as well as my country, as well as my planet, who are able to do so many things that I can't *and are doing them*! Still, I have no interest in spending time regretting what I can't do. The question is always, what *can* I do?

For one thing, I can write with a modest amount of coherence. So, I can write this book, all royalties for which will go to charity.

What else can I do? I'm retired, widowed, and without children – so my financial needs are not huge. I can and do make continuing contributions to charities that are particularly stressed in this time of need – with most of those contributions going to local, state, and worldwide food and health organizations (as examples: the "Nourishing Network", my local school district's lunch program while school is no longer in session; "Northwest Harvest" which works to provide food for people in Washington; and "Doctors Without Borders" which works worldwide to deal with health issues, be they food, medical or other). This I can do.

More than that, at my age I've met a lot of people. I have a pretty extensive phonebook. I can call people I know, even if I haven't spoken to them in a while (or even a *long* while!) and catch up. A lot of us are feeling intensely isolated. A phone call is a wonderful way to reach out. And even though I'm pretty much of an introvert, I can pick up the flaming phone and call people. That I can do.

One thing I've learned that I'd like to pass along is that if we truly ask how someone is, if we're truly interested in how they are doing, they will tell us. I've had hour-long conversations with folks where I've mostly listened.

A quick sharing of an observation. Our culture spends very little time teaching us how to listen. Much too often, it seems that we tend to think of conversations as a game of ping-pong. You whack the ball to my side. I whack it back to yours. Then you whack it back to mine. This can make for a good match, but I'm not convinced that it makes for a good conversation. As a simple example, let's imagine you say "I saw a movie last night. *Son of X.*" If my reply is, "I didn't have a chance to watch a movie last night. I was too busy." then the ping-pong match is on. But let's imagine that instead I say, "*Son of X.* I don't think I know that film. Did you like it? Tell me about it." Now, instead of a ping-pong match, we actually have at least the beginning of a conversation. All this to suggest not only that we call people, but that we truly reach out to folks and have conversations. And for me, the foundation of a good conversation is listening.

These are things that I can do. They happen to be the cards I have. I'm offering them simply as examples. What's important is for each of us to examine our own cards and then act to play those cards in the most positive way we can.

As one more example, there was a time I gave blood regularly. I can't anymore, but if you can, there is, as I write this, a national shortage of blood in our country. If one of your cards is the ability to give blood, it's a bloody important card (sorry: I couldn't resist).

Another amazing thing, or so it seems to me, is that sometimes by doing for ourselves we are also able help others. Is that cool or what? One example of this is a ritual I shared earlier, something so important to me that I do it every day to try to keep myself centered. I post a "Good morning, world" on Facebook every morning, and an "Evening smile" before shutting down my computer every night. I do this for me. I do this because (long story, please just accept it here) I can't visualize worth a darn. I post the good morning and evening smile on my page because if I don't post it, I can't see it! What is cool is that I've heard from so many friends how much they look forward to the "Good morning" and "Evening smile". It helps them too! So, in doing something for me, I've done something for my friends as well. This isn't always the case, but it sure warms the heart when it is.

To conclude this chapter, here is a quick reminder that in the last chapter we talked about beginning each day, asking:

1) What can I do for me *today*?

2) What can I do for my family and friends *today*?

3) What can I do for my human family *today*?

This brings us to remembering that we have two families we want to "do" for. One is our immediate family. The other is for our human family. Sometimes we become so involved in doing for one family that we forget the other. Again, we seek balance, which is why I really do suggest we ask ourselves these questions every day. Or, heck, every other day. Or at least three times a week. Whatever works! I rarely if ever want to speak in absolutes. Always, we want to seek what works for us, what helps us. What works for me may not be helpful for you – not because one of us is "better" or "worse" but because we're human – we're all different. The bottom line is facing both this pandemic and the huge strain it has placed on our lives. How we keep our balance is up to us. What IS important to remember is that each of us is important. So yes, I need to do for me; but not to the exclusion of you, nor the exclusion of those who don't look like me, or see the holy as I do, or live on "my" side of those artificial lines we draw on maps called borders.

Seeking Balance In an Unbalanced Time

Remembering more of the words of Reverend Hale, "I am only one, but I am one. I cannot do everything, but I can do something." The "something" each of us can do will be different. What remains important, indeed crucial, particularly in a time of crisis, is that we do what we can. The hope of this small book is to help us think about what it is we can do: and then move us to do it, whatever form what we can do may take.

Which brings us to our final chapter. It's something we can do that may not occur to us in this time of clear and immediate crisis. I hope we might at least begin to ponder what we want our future to look like, because our future will be upon us before we know it. I deeply believe that we owe it to posterity to get at least a little ahead of the curve.

Steven Greenebaum

4

Envisioning and Working for Our Future

The point of this brief concluding chapter is not to attempt to provide answers. Rather, things are so intense and so difficult right now that it can be hard even to think of the future. Yet with everything so upside down, I believe we have an important opportunity to consider what we want to see in the future. A "new normal" is going to come out of this. How do we want that to look? It's, of course, very human for us to shrug and say, "This just isn't the time for that." But as Hillel would remind us, "If not now, when?"

There will be a new normal. There's no disputing that. Do we simply want to stumble into it? Or do our children and their children deserve better? I have no children. But I care about yours. And I deeply believe they deserve a healthy "new normal".

So, what I'd ask of us now is for us to begin pondering some questions. Below are just a few that occur to me. What's important are not these questions to the exclusion of others, but rather that we take the time, even now, to think of the future and to do what we can to enter that future with intent rather than simply by chance.

1) As the pandemic recedes, what do we want the world to look like?

2) Was the "old normal" so wonderful that we simply want to try to regain it? If not, what would we want changed?

3) Are companies more important than the people who work there? If not, what would we want changed?

4) With so many dying in nursing homes, do we need to rethink how we treat our seniors?

5) Is the Climate Crisis something that we need to address? And if so, what should we be changing in how we live as we embrace our "new normal"?

6) Are we at last ready to deal with racism? If so, how can we best embrace the whole of our human family?

There are so many other questions. These six are just intended to get the ball rolling. What I deeply believe is so very important is that we begin to think about our world "after the pandemic" so we might be more intentional about what that world looks like.

Finally, following this chapter is an Appendix that I hope the reader will find helpful. It includes some thoughts others have offered in difficult times that have been important to me in my life. It also includes some thoughts of my own that I have written over the past several years that helped me to focus.

Know that I wish you well. Know that you are important. Know that we all are family. Take care. We are in this together.

Appendix
Thoughts in a Time of Crisis

THOUGHTS FROM OTHERS
THAT I HAVE LONG VALUED

"I am only one, but I am one. I cannot do everything, but I can do something. And because I cannot do everything, I will not refuse to do the something that I can do."

Rev. Edward Everett Hale (1882-1902)—This comes with slight variations in the wording, and as far as I can tell there is no "definitive" version. But the essence of it is always the same and hugely important.

"You are not obligated to complete the work, but neither are you free to desist from it."

Rabbi Tarfon (writing around 120 CE)—Offers those of us who feel the work before us is impossibly huge, some important, reassuring, and empowering words.

Steven Greenebaum

A FEW POSSIBLY HELPFUL POEMS/
MEDITATIONS

If I can stop one Heart from breaking,
I shall not live in vain
If I can ease one Life the Aching,
Or cool one Pain,
Or help one fainting Robin
Unto his Nest again,
I shall not live in vain.

Emily Dickinson (Poems by Emily Dickinson, 1890)

No man is an island,
Entire of itself.
Each is a piece of the continent,
A part of the main.
If a clod be washed away by the sea,
Europe is the less.
As well as if a promontory were.
As well as if a manor of thine own
Or of thine friend's were.
Any man's death diminishes me,
For I am involved in mankind.
Therefore, send not to know
For whom the bell tolls,
It tolls for thee.

John Donne (1624 Meditation 17)

Take kindly the counsel of the years,
gracefully surrendering the things of youth.
Nurture strength of spirit to shield you in sudden

misfortune.
But do not distress yourself with dark imaginings.
Many fears are born of fatigue and loneliness.
Beyond a wholesome discipline, be gentle with
yourself.

You are a child of the universe, no less than the
trees and the stars;
you have a right to be here.
And whether or not it is clear to you,
no doubt the universe is unfolding as it should.

Therefore be at peace with God, whatever you
conceive Him to be,
and whatever your labors and aspirations, in the
noisy confusion of life keep peace with your soul.

With all its sham, drudgery, and broken dreams,
it is still a beautiful world.
Be cheerful. Strive to be happy.

> Max Ehrmann (*Desiderata*, 1948) This is the last third
> of a lengthy meditation. The full work is available on the
> web.

I cannot say how I will die,
But I decide how I shall live.
I do not know what I will get,
But mine the knowledge I can give.

For love's a gift that's born within
And shows the other pleasures pale.
Though mist enclouds what fate may bring,
The life is mine, I cannot fail.

> Steven Greenebaum (*One Family: Indivisible*, 2019)

SOME POSSIBLY HELPFUL
THOUGHTS ALONG THE WAY

It is not a sign of weakness to say, "I don't know."
It is weakness to say we know when we don't.

Hate and intolerance are cancers. Our Scriptures
tell us to love our neighbor as much to protect us
as to protect our neighbor.

Family matters—both my immediate family and
my human family. If I would keep my balance, I
must not neglect either.

Who we are is indistinguishable from how we
treat what we consider "other."

The most important thing in life is not making a
living; it's making a difference. Help a neighbor.
Make a difference.

Fear is virulent, mind-numbing, and contagious.
There are indeed bad people, but whoever tells us
to fear the other seeks to enslave us.

There will be days when I cannot keep myself
from anger, but I can keep from acting on it.
There will be days when I feel frustrated,

but I can keep from withdrawing because of it.
Love and justice guide me.
My course is steady even when winds and
darkness challenge.

If we say, "I hate this, but there's nothing I can
do,"
we are complicit.
If we say, "This is terrible, but it's just not my
problem,"
we are complicit.
Some of us can do big things, some of us medium-
sized things,
some of us small things;
But *all* of us can do something.
Our family needs us.

Ignore the propaganda. Success in life is not
about winning. It is about walking our path with
justice, compassion, and humility. Your success is
inextricably tied to mine. My success is inextricably tied to yours. To the extent we forget or ignore
this, we have lost our way.

May love and conscience be our companions.
May justice be our guiding star.

Compassion is an act of love.
Pity is an act of privilege.

Let us not confuse the two.
Compassion compels us to act.
Pity allows us to sit back and feel superior.

Despair is to surrender. No matter how dark the
clouds, let us light a candle. Let us engage darkness with love and unrelenting light.

I am not the whole of me. *We*, every shade, every
gender, every ethnicity, every spiritual path, *we*
are all a part of the whole. If I would be whole, I
must embrace *us*.

Hope without action is self-deluding.
Action without hope is just anger.
Let us be hopeful and relentlessly active.

May we not grieve overlong what we have lost,
Remain curious about what we may yet find,
And be grateful for what we have.

Lack of confidence is not humility. Humility is a
byproduct of confidence and self-knowledge. Self-
importance is a byproduct of insecurity.

When we tire, and we will, let us remember that
we are called not only to love our neighbor as

ourselves but to love ourselves as we love our
neighbor. Take a breath, and remember we are
one family. Your family needs you!

Religion can be used to engage our humanity
or to avoid it. If our religious beliefs point us to
"me and mine, us vs. them," we are avoiding our
humanity. To paraphrase Kennedy, ask not what
humanity can do for us, ask what we can do for
our human family.

In these hugely difficult times,
If we give in to anger, we become its prisoner.
Yet if we do not stay engaged, we become irrel-
evant.
Let us seek balance.

Buddhist, Christian, Muslim, Jew, Hindu, Pagan,
Humanist, or any other spiritual path: it is not the
ethics we espouse that matters. What matters are
the ethics we live.

We build prisons for ourselves with bricks of arro-
gance and bars of fear. It is self-enslavement. May
we embrace and help to create an era of fearless
humility. Only then will we truly be free.

We are in this together. Even as we are apart, we are in this together.
It is when we turn inward and think only of ourselves that our soul dies. Let us reach out to one another!

The only folks who never stumble
Are those too afraid to walk.
So, keep walking.
And when we stumble, let us remember to smile.

Today, I rest.
I rest not because there is nothing to do
But because I can do nothing if I will not rest.
My body, my mind, my soul demand rest.
With so much to do, let me never forget
I cannot do if I will not rest.

ONE FAMILY INDIVISIBLE
A SPIRITUAL MEMOIR

One Family: Indivisible is truly a great read ...
genuinely captivating and brilliant.
— Ron Irwin, *Splash Magazines*

Can interfaith mean more than respectful dia-
logue or theological tolerance? Steven Greenebaum's spiritual memoir, *One Family: Indivisible*, gives us a resounding yes. His life-journey
brought him to the realization that interfaith
is a way of believing and living — a profound,
inclusive encounter with the mystery of the
Holy. This book and his founding ministry are
a promise of hope for all spiritual seekers."
— Father John Heagle, priest, counselor, author

"Unreservedly recommended... especially
recommended for the personal reading lists of
seekers from all races, ethnicities, and spiritual
paths who are searching for that elusive goal
of a community of love and inclusion that also
respect social, cultural, racial, economic, and
political diversity in harmony" — *Midwest
Book Review*.

MSI Press

Books in Our Pandemic Series